Growth Mindset Grit For Kids

Adrian Laurent

Copyright © 2021 by Adrian Laurent

All rights reserved. No part of this book may be reproduced or used in any manner without written permission of the copyright owner except for the use of quotations in a book review.

Limit of Liability/Disclaimer of Warranty:
This is a work of fiction. Names, characters, places, and incidents either are the product of the author's imagination or are used fictitiously. Any resemblance to actual persons, living or dead, events, or locales is entirely coincidental.

Although the publisher and the author have made every effort to ensure that the information in this book was correct at press time and while this publication is designed to provide accurate information in regard to the subject matter covered, the publisher and the author assume no responsibility for errors, inaccuracies, omissions, or any other inconsistencies herein and hereby disclaim any liability to any party for any loss, damage, or disruption caused by errors or omissions, whether such errors or omissions result from negligence, accident, or any other cause.

The information in this book is not intended to be used, nor should be used, to diagnose or treat any mental health or medical condition. For diagnosis or treatment of any mental health or medical condition, consult a licensed professional, psychologist or physician. Both the author and publisher of this book are not liable or responsible for any damages or negative consequences from any preparation, treatment, action, application to any person.

ISBN 978-0-473-58780-2 (paperback)
ISBN 978-0-473-58781-9 (epub)

Bradem Press
New Zealand
2021
www.adrianlaurent.com

Jack loved to watch his Mommy race. She raced in triathlons. First you swim, then a bike ride, and then they run to the finish.

Jack saw a sign. There was going to be a race for kids Jack's age. A triathlon, with swimming, cycling and running.
He could be in a race just like his Mom!

Jack asked if he could do it. It was just a few weeks away, and Mommy was already signed up for the grown-ups' race.

Mommy said Jack could race, but would need to practice swimming, bike-riding and running. Jack was thrilled! He could not wait to race just like Mommy!

They went to the pool to practice swimming. Mommy needed to train for her race too, so Grandpa came to help.

Mommy jumped in the pool and started swimming, she sped off so fast! Jack wanted to do that.

Jack got in the water. He was always happy splashing and playing, but hadn't swam far before. He started to swim to the other end of the pool.

He got tired quickly. It was really tough, and it took ages to get to the other side.

Jack was sad, he wanted to be fast just like his Mommy.

He started to pedal, was okay for a bit, but then the path went uphill, and it got really hard.

Grandpa ran to Jack. "Are you alright, Jack?" He asked.
"It's not fair." Said Jack. "Why can't I be as fast as Mommy?"
"Oh Jack, that's because you're at the start of your journey."

Jack kept swimming every day. It was hard at first, but then he started to improve.

Jack rode his bike as well. He got better at that too.

On the day of the race, Jack was nervous but excited. He and the other kids lined up, then BANG! The race began.

Jack didn't look at anyone else, just jumped straight in the water and started swimming.

He could hear his Mommy and Grandpa cheering as he got out of the water and got on to his bike.

He rode as fast as he could. He was tired, but kept going, like he practiced.

Then it was time to run. Jack ran everywhere all the time! So even though he was exhausted, he felt happy to be running. He saw the finish line ahead!

Jack couldn't believe it. His practice had paid off. Mommy and Grandpa lifted him in the air. He was a champion racer, just like his Mommy.

www.ingramcontent.com/pod-product-compliance
Lightning Source LLC
Chambersburg PA
CBHW041203290426
44109CB00003B/115